The Portable
USB Blender
Smoothie
BOOK

101 "On the Go" Smoothies for Your Travel Blender!

By Lisa Brian

HHF Press
San Francisco

CONTENTS

WHY YOU NEED THIS BOOK   1

WHY SMOOTHIES?   4

SMOOTHIES CAN HELP YOU HEAL   7

HOW TO USE YOUR USB BLENDER   10

PRO TIPS FOR MAKING AMAZING SMOOTHIES   12

HOW TO USE THIS BOOK   15

ANTI – AGING   17

    Anti-Ultra Violet   18

    Berry Nice Indeed   19

    Green is Keen   20

    Green Tea Coconut Strawberry   21

    Kale Delight   22

    Kale is Queen   23

    Minty Coconut Blueberry   24

    Peachy Blueberry   25

    Pineapple Express   26

    Pineapple Mango   27

    Pure Gold   28

    Relax   29

    Wake Up   30

    Wrinkle Be Gone   31

BONES & JOINTS   32

    Osteo Punch   33

    Strong Bones   34

CONSTIPATION   35

    Epsom Salt Surprise   36

    Prune   37

DETOX   38

    Algae for Everyone   39

    Avo-Cucumber   40

    Beet This   41

    Berry Minty Apple   42

    Blue Ginger   43

    Cilantro Detox   44

    Cranberry, Cranberry   45

Cucumber Kale   46
Detox Berry   47
Feel Good   48
Fiberlicious   49
Goji Goodness   50
Jicama Surprise   51
Kale/Mango Detox   52
Smooth As Silk   53
Spicy Carrot   54
Spirulina Special Source   55
Super Cleanse   56
Sweet Fruit Detox Special   57
Tangy Blueberry   58
Zesty Apple   59

BLOOD SUGAR   **60**
Kale-Apple   61
Zesty Lime   62

IMMUNE SYSTEM   **63**
Avocado   64
Granny Green   65
The Cold Fighter   66

BEAUTY   **67**
Romantic Veggie   68
Royal Avocado   69

ENERGY-BOOST   **70**
Berry Burst   71
Green Goblin   72
Mean Green Machine   73

HEALTH   **74**
Apple Caramel   75
Delicious Banana Cream   76
Banana Pumpkin   77
Berry Carrot   78
Berry-Granate   79
Cafe Banana   80
Chocolate Divine   81
Chocolatey Date   82
Coconut Almond   83
Flaxseed Spinach   84
Green Tea Banana   85

KC Delight (Kale/Coconut) ... 86
Lemon Strawberry ... 87
Minty Spinach ... 88
PB&J ... 89
Raisin Bliss ... 90
Smoothie Sundae ... 91
Spunky Monkey ... 92
Strawberry Peach ... 93
Veggie Spice ... 94
Melonberry ... 95

HEART ... 96

Flaxseed Supreme ... 97
Hardy Heart ... 98
Pomegranate Pump ... 99

MOOD ... 100

Good Mood Oatmeal ... 101
Happy Green ... 102
Up, Up and Away ... 103

PERFORMANCE ... 104

Oatmeal ... 105
Peanut Butter Banana ... 106

STRESS ... 107

Banana-Berry ... 108
Grapefruit-Kale ... 109
Mint-Fennel-Pineapple ... 110

WEIGHT LOSS ... 111

Apple Pie ... 112
Avocado Fiesta ... 113
Avocado - Swiss Chard ... 114
Banana - Choco Split ... 115
Banana Peanut Butter Delight ... 116
Berry Berry Yummy ... 117
Blue Smoothie ... 118
Cashew Banana ... 119
Citrus Joy ... 120
Grab Bag ... 121
Hawaiian Supreme ... 122
Kale-Ginger ... 123
Hot Tomato ... 124
Key Lime ... 125

Mango Bliss   126
Melon Perfection   127
Mocha Espresso Wake Up   128
Peachy Keen   129
Raspberry Treat   130
Red Banana   131
Strawberry Spinach   132
Tooty-Fruity   133

KIDS   **134**

Ice Cream-Less   135
Peanut Butter Madness   136
The Hybrid   137

Want a Personal 24/7 Cooking Coach?

Learn New Recipes & Techniques for FREE!

Get Access Now!
Go to www.CookingCoach.online
or use this QR code:

CHAPTER 1
Why You Need This Book

The Only Book Written for USB Blenders

This book is specifically written for people who own or use a USB personal blender. Why? Because your USB blender requires smaller portions and may not have the power of a countertop blender. Do you travel a lot and want to maximize your USB blender's use? Then this book is for you!

Smoothie "Remedies" for Many Common Health Conditions

Do you suffer from low energy? Or do you need to improve your hair, eyesight or waistline? This book is written in a way to provide specific smoothie suggestions for many of the health conditions most of us face through our lives. Just look up a health condition in the table of contents, and flip to the recipes that are suggested to help. This book does not offer medical advice—only your doctor can provide medical advice. Instead, this book offers common sense suggestions which may help based on the nutrients each recipe contains.

101 of The Most Beneficial and Delicious Smoothie Recipes

This informative book gives you enough recipes to last several months, offering a different smoothie recipe each day. Of course, if you mix and match, and experiment with the recipes, you can have a different smoothie each day for 365 days in a year. These recipes are designed specifically for your durable and long-lasting compact, personal blender. All recipes are kitchen-tested for taste and categorized for your specific and general health needs.

Pro Nutritional Tips About Superfood Smoothie Ingredients

Become a smoothie expert! Besides getting healthier each day by using your blender to make delicious meal replacement smoothies, the nutritional tips in this book will make you more aware of what you're eating, and will emphasize the nutritional benefits of each smoothie you whip up. You'll also become a healthy smoothie expert once you learn about all the vital and essential nutrients that your smoothies have in them.

It's The Only Smoothie Book You'll Ever Need

This book is a perfect companion to your USB blender. It is so complete that you won't need to buy another smoothie book as long as you own your blender, which could be a long, long time. It covers the nutritional aspects of your smoothies, along with all the "how to's" you can think of. This book should be kept in the kitchen because you'll probably use it on a daily basis.

CHAPTER 2
Why Smoothies?

Smoothies make sure nothing is wasted. When you blend fruits and vegetables in your blender, the fiber, as well as every single bit of produce you put in, is blended to a perfectly smooth consistency. This process unlocks all the nutrients and makes it easier and quicker for the body to absorb them. Traditional juicers and blenders simply cut up the greens and the fruit, and give you only a small percentage of the juice that is actually within the fruit itself. They also leave a lot of the fiber in a solid state, which is then discarded by the unfortunate juicer owner.

Smoothies Aid in the Battle to Lose Weight

Anyone who has ever tasted a fruit smoothie knows that they are a delicious way to get lots of vital nutrition for the body. They also know that they felt better almost immediately after consumption, and had more energy than usual. Another benefit of fruit smoothies is a feeling of fullness and satisfaction for several hours after savoring the fabulous drink. Many of the smoothie recipes in this book have been designed for weight loss. They can be used as meal replacers and are ultra-delicious while also keeping you full and energetic for hours at a time.

How long does a traditional breakfast of pancakes, eggs and sausage take to cook? Probably a lot longer than anyone in today's modern culture would like. You have to make the pancake batter, heat the skillet, fry the eggs, and fry the sausages, all of which probably takes at least half an hour. How long does it take to make a delicious tasting, meal replacing, protein and nutrient-packed smoothie? Throw the washed veggies and fruit into the blender along with protein powder, honey, yogurt, soy milk and whatever else you feel like putting in there, and you'll have a nutritious breakfast in under five minutes. Plus, you have made the very healthy decision to skip the greasy, fat-filled, high cholesterol conventional breakfast that will leave you feeling heavy and tired over the next few hours.

CHAPTER 3
Smoothies Can Help You Heal

We are all grateful when we get an extra burst of energy. Coffee and other caffeinated drinks, along with sugary snacks give us these bursts, but they don't last very long and the come down is always at the wrong time. Fruit smoothies, on the other hand, can give us a steady flow of natural energy that lasts for hours at a time. Fruits and vegetables have amazing nutritional properties. When the fruits and veggies are broken down to their most absorbable size, you're getting all the energy and nutrients that you need to feel your best. Fruit and veggie smoothies provide healthful and reliable energy for athletes, students, homemakers, business people and everyone who simply needs more stamina.

Smoothies Add More Fiber to Your Diet

By using a blender to break down vegetables and fruits, you can add more fiber (roughage), to your diet. Fiber can aid digestion, promote weight loss, reduce the risk of heart disease, colon cancer, diabetes and strokes. Consuming smoothies will increase the intake of fiber to your diet and will begin to flush toxins from your body. It will also give you a feeling of fullness, which means that you will naturally want to eat less and consequently lose weight.

Smoothies Provide Antioxidants to Prevent or Delay Cell Damage

Antioxidants are simply chemicals in the body that block the negative activity of other chemicals known as free radicals. Free radicals cause damage to our cells, which could lead to cancer. The body naturally produces free radicals, and fruit smoothies are a great way to fight them. Our smoothie recipes contain a great deal of fruits and vegetables, which are high in antioxidants that fight against these free radicals. There are plenty of fruits which contain anti-oxidants, such as blueberries, blackberries, strawberries, apples, kale, carrots and beets.

Smoothies Enable You to Lose Weight

A smoothie per day keeps the pounds away. We coined that phrase because it's true! When you replace a meal with a smoothie, you can't help but lose weight. You're getting a healthy meal in a glass instead of a long sit-down meal full of sugar, salt and refined, indigestible who knows what that will take a day or more to digest. The meal replacement smoothie gives you what your body needs in a delicious and easily digestible manner, which will help you lose those pounds right away.

Smoothies Are an Easy Way to Get Superfoods into Your Body

Superfoods are special foods in a category all by themselves. They are extremely high in nutrients and generally low in calories, which can improve your mental and physical health. We made sure to put lots of superfoods in our smoothie recipes including blueberries, kale, beets, sweet potatoes, swiss chard, spinach, chia seeds and flax seeds. These smoothie recipes make it easy for anyone to ingest lots of superfoods in a quick, delicious way.

CHAPTER 4

How to Use Your USB Blender

Your Blender and Its Capabilities

A USB personal blender is handy on the go or in the office! It's small, which makes it easy to take with you. Don't let the size fool you though, since it's capable of making so many things. Salsas and soups are a breeze to make in your compact blender. You can also make sauces and homemade dressing with ease. You'll have no problem making all of your favorite recipes right at home. As you will soon find out, your blender makes delicious smoothies, but we're also going to show you how to do so much more than that.

One Speed for All Jobs

Your blender takes all the guesswork out of which speed to use. You simply place it on the base, turn it on, and it does all the work for you. You can also pulse the mixture if you need a more controlled chop for sauces such as salsa. Simply push down the cup onto the base for your desired time, instead of turning it. The blender will stop blending when you are no longer pushing down. It's that easy.

Easy Clean Up

Here's a quick tip to clean your blender quickly: put all of the cups on the top shelf of the dishwasher, and wash on the normal setting. If you don't have a dishwasher, fill the cup about two thirds full with warm water and add a drop or two of dish soap. Screw on the milling blades, and blend for 20 to 30 seconds. Rinse out the cups and dry with a towel. Never place the blade in the dishwasher. This will dull the blade. Always hand wash the blade assembly with warm, soapy water. If you need to clean the base, simply wipe it down with a wet towel when it's unplugged.

CHAPTER 5
Pro Tips for Making Amazing Smoothies

LIQUID – For an even texture and consistency of your smoothie, you should add half of the liquid at the beginning and half at the end.

PROTEIN POWDER – Add this ingredient next, right after the first liquid is poured into the blender. Powders thicken your smoothie and give it a creamy texture. When you add it early on, the powder will blend a lot easier and won't end up with a chalky quality to it.

NUTS, BERRIES, FLAX SEEDS, SWEETENERS AND PEANUT OR ALMOND BUTTERS – These blend in very well with the rest of the smoothie ingredients when they are in the middle of the blender mixture.

LEAFY GREENS – Add the leafy greens next. If you add these at the beginning or at the end, they may oxidize and lose some of their nutrients. They will also not be pulverized completely and there will be chunks of the leaves left in the smoothie.

FROZEN FRUIT – Adding frozen fruit after veggies keep the greens cool and enables the frozen fruit to blend much more efficiently.

ICE – Always add ice last. This will keep your greens and other foods from overheating and give your smoothie a cool and thick composition.

LIQUID – After blending for a few moments, add the rest of the liquid and finish blending. This will give you the best quality blend you can get in a smoothie.

Should You Use Fresh or Frozen Fruit?

Fresh is always the best for optimal nutrition. Plus, the taste is extraordinary compared to frozen. The benefits of frozen fruit, however, are still incredible. The old saying about the levels of nutrition is: fresh is best, then frozen, then canned. Frozen fruit in a smoothie is a tradition that will never die, and there's no need for it to go away. Frozen fruit keeps your smoothie cool and makes it thicker.

Extracting Hidden Nutrition from Whole Fruits and Vegetables

One of the best things about a compact blender is that it utilizes the whole fruit and vegetable. It doesn't leave a pile of fibrous waste, which includes valuable nutrients and fiber. Compact blenders are purposely designed to extract ALL of the nutrients in each piece of fruit and vegetable you use. Other juicers and blenders are constructed to break down only the least difficult parts of the vegetables and fruit. They just don't have the strength and extracting power of a compact blender, which is capable of completely breaking down ingredients and extracting every possible nutrient.

Prepare Portions Ahead of Time

If you love smoothies, it might serve you to prepare some of your ingredients ahead of time. That way, when you feel like having a smoothie, most of the work is already done. You can slice bananas, strawberries and any other fruit you may want in your smoothie, put them in a freezer bag and pop them into the freezer. Prep time will be cut in half (or more), and you can have a delicious smoothie in just a minute or two. Freezing carrots or beets or other hard vegetables, along with lettuce or dandelion greens is not recommended. These vegetables might end up too hard and could damage the blender.

Thickening Trick

If you add too much liquid to your smoothie, try adding a bit yogurt, oatmeal, avocado, banana or even chia seeds to thicken it up.

Storing Smoothies for Later

Make a double batch so you'll have a smoothie for later! Just store your extra smoothie in a glass container (Mason Jars are very good for this), with an airtight lid to keep it fresh. Fill it to the very top just to make sure no air gets inside. Professional smoothie makers always add a few drops of lemon juice to their smoothie because that extra vitamin C keeps it from oxidizing

CHAPTER 6
How to Use This Book

This book was written to make it easy for you to get the most out of your USB blender. We've developed over a hundred delicious recipes that are exclusive to compact blenders and their owners. We've grouped these recipes into easy to find and even easier to read categories that focus on maintaining general vitality and targeting specific health concerns.

Smoothies for Health Conditions

These smoothie recipes deal with specific topics that many people are interested in.

These smoothies all have unique ingredients that focus on targeted ailments and have shown to produce the desired results.

IMPORTANT: The smoothies and their ingredients are not cures to any illnesses, and we are not claiming that they are. The ingredients used in these particular smoothies have worked to improve the health and wellbeing of millions of people, and when taken in smoothie form, are easily digestible and quite delicious.

Some of the recipes are categorized as such:

- Anti-Aging Smoothies
- Bone and Joints Smoothies
- Constipation Smoothies
- Detox Smoothies
- Blood Sugar Smoothies
- Immune System Smoothies
- Lifestyle Smoothies

This section of the book has recipes that can address specific health concerns in one's life and health. The ingredients have been used by millions of people all around the world for generations and can have a highly beneficial outcome on the human body.

Some of the recipes in this section include:

- Beauty Smoothies
- Energy Smoothies
- Health Smoothies
- Heart Smoothies
- Kid Smoothies
- Mood Smoothies
- Performance Smoothies
- Stress Smoothies
- Weight Loss Smoothies

CHAPTER 7
Anti - Aging

Anti-Ultra Violet

Now you can help fight the negative effects of the sun on your skin from the inside out. This doesn't replace sunscreen, but it will help protect your sensitive skin from the sun's harmful ultra violet rays.

INGREDIENTS

- 1 1/4 cups coconut water
- 1 1/4 oranges (sliced, peeled and seeded)
- 1 kiwi (peeled and sliced)
- 1 tablespoon flaxseeds (preferably ground or in powder form)

DIRECTIONS

1. Place all of the ingredients in your blender, and blend for about 30 seconds, or until desired consistency is reached.

Nutritional Info: Calories: 189 | Sodium: 275mg | Dietary Fiber: 9.9 | Total Fat: 3.3g | Total Carbs: 36.8 | Protein: 5.2g.

Berry Nice Indeed

SERVINGS: 1

This is jam packed with antioxidants! Combined with the vitamin C and E from the blueberries and strawberries, the Omega-3 from the flaxseeds make this a great anti-aging formula that will fight wrinkles and help your skin to glow.

INGREDIENTS

2 ounces strawberries
3 ounces blueberries
1/4 avocado
1 teaspoon ground flaxseed
1/2 cup ice cubes

DIRECTIONS

1. Place all of the ingredients in your blender, and blend for about 30 seconds, or until desired consistency is reached.

Nutritional Info: Calories: 105 | Sodium: 3mg | Dietary Fiber: 4.3g | Total Fat: 6.4g | Total Carbs: 11.8g | Protein: 1.7g.

Green is Keen

This simple drink can do wonders for your skin and health in general. There is a great deal of natural vitamin E and C in these ingredients, which are highly beneficial to your skin and to your overall beauty.

INGREDIENTS

3/4 bananas
3/4 cups spinach (chopped)
1-ounce avocado (peeled and pit removed)
1 tablespoon sunflower seeds
1-ounce lemon juice (no seeds)
1 1/4 cups soy or almond milk (low fat dairy milk is okay too)
1 1/2 tablespoons sweetener (your choice)

DIRECTIONS

1. Place all of the ingredients in your blender, and blend for about 30 seconds, or until desired consistency is reached.

Nutritional Info: Calories: 331 | Sodium: 52mg | Dietary Fiber: 8.4g | Total Fat: 13g | Total Carbs: 46.9g | Protein: 8g.

Green Tea Coconut Strawberry

The ingredients in this smoothie will help keep your weight down and enhance your digestion, while giving a youthful glow to your skin.

INGREDIENTS

- 1 tablespoon green tea powder
- 3/4 bananas
- 1 1/2 cups strawberries
- 1 cup coconut water
- 1 1/2 tablespoons chia seeds
- 1/8 cup plain yogurt
- 1 tablespoon sweetener (honey or sweetener of your choice)

DIRECTIONS

1. Place all of the ingredients in your blender, and blend for about 30 seconds, or until desired consistency is reached.

Nutritional Info: Calories: 220 | Sodium: 188mg | Dietary Fiber: 11g | Total Fat: 2.9g | Total Carbs: 48.6g | Protein: 5.9g.

Kale Delight

Plenty of zinc and A and C vitamins here, along with calcium and other necessary minerals to keep your blood healthy, and infections and colds away.

INGREDIENTS

- 1/2 banana
- 1/2 cup kale leaves (or collard greens or bok choy)
- 1/8 cup pitted dates
- 1/2 cup arugula
- 1/2 cup milk (soy or almond milk OK)

DIRECTIONS

1. Place all of the ingredients in your blender, and blend for about 30 seconds, or until desired consistency is reached.

Nutritional Info: Calories: 176 | Sodium: 61mg | Dietary Fiber: 4.0g | Total Fat: 0.6g | Total Carbs: 39.9g | Protein: 6.5g.

Kale is Queen

Kale is the queen of the superfoods. This leafy green is packed with vitamins and minerals, and is considered by many to be one of the best antioxidant-packed food in the world. It's great for detoxes, lowering cholesterol and it's super for your digestive and urinary systems.

INGREDIENTS

- 1 carrot (cleaned and chopped)
- 1 cup kale (leaves only, no stems)
- 1 1/4 cups coconut water
- 1 1/4 apples (green preferably)
- 1/8 cup lemon juice

DIRECTIONS

1. Place all of the ingredients in your blender, and blend for about 30 seconds, or until desired consistency is reached.

Nutritional Info: Calories: 158 | Sodium: 239mg | Dietary Fiber: 6g | Total Fat: 0.7g | Total Carbs: 36.2g | Protein: 4.2g.

Minty Coconut Blueberry

This smoothie sounds like it tastes: delicious! It also supplies your body with a great deal of vitamin C to help maintain your health and youthful appearance. The chia seeds will keep you feeling full for hours, which could lead to weight loss..

INGREDIENTS

- 1 1/4 cups coconut water
- 3/4 cups blueberries
- 3/4 cups strawberries
- 1 teaspoon chia seeds
- 1/8 cup leaves of mint
- 1 tablespoon lemon juice

DIRECTIONS

1. Place all of the ingredients in your blender, and blend for about 30 seconds, or until desired consistency is reached.

Nutritional Info: Calories: 178 | Sodium: 258mg | Dietary Fiber: 10g | Total Fat: 2.4g | Total Carbs: 37.3 | Protein: 4.9g.

Peachy Blueberry

This smoothie is not only sweet and delicious, but it's loaded with plenty of vitamin C and E which promote youthful looking skin and hair—not to mention the many benefits to your overall health.

INGREDIENTS

- 1 cup low fat milk or almond or soy milk
- 1 cup sliced peaches (fresh is best, then frozen, then canned)
- 1/2 cup blueberries
- 1 tablespoon sweetener of choice (optional)

DIRECTIONS

1. Add sweetener of choice, if desired.
2. Place all of the ingredients in your blender, and blend for about 30 seconds, or until desired consistency is reached.

Nutritional Info: Calories: 203 | Sodium: 108mg | Dietary Fiber: 4.1 | Total Fat: 3g | Total Carbs: 36.7g | Protein: 10.2g.

Pineapple Express

SERVINGS: 1

Pineapples, mangoes, kale and coconut water all have wonderful nutrients that contribute to a more youthful and healthy appearance. Your newly glowing and hydrated skin will probably be the first thing you'll notice once you start mixing these smoothies on a regular basis.

INGREDIENTS

- 1 cup pineapple chunks
- 3/4 cups mango chunks
- 1 cup coconut water
- 3/4 cups kale (chopped)
- 1 tablespoon chia seeds

DIRECTIONS

1. Place all of the ingredients in your blender, and blend for about 30 seconds, or until desired consistency is reached.

Nutritional Info: Calories: 256 | Sodium: 142mg | Dietary Fiber: 11.5g | Total Fat: 3.4g | Total Carbs: 54.1g | Protein: 7g.

Pineapple Mango

This incredibly simple drink with only a few basic ingredients has the potential to transform your health and your skin. Plenty of vitamins, minerals and Omega-3s in this recipe.

INGREDIENTS

- 3/4 cups pineapple chunks
- 1/2 cup mango chunks
- 1 1/4 cups coconut water
- 1 tablespoon chia seeds

DIRECTIONS

1. Place all of the ingredients in your blender, and blend for about 30 seconds, or until desired consistency is reached.

Nutritional Info: Calories: 215 | Sodium: 272mg | Dietary Fiber: 11.1g | Total Fat: 3.7g | Total Carbs: 42.8g | Protein: 6g.

Pure Gold

This smoothie is full of antioxidants and will keep you looking and feeling young. The ginger, with its immune boosting and cleansing effects, will also help you flush the unwanted toxins out of your body.

INGREDIENTS

- 1/4 carrot, sliced
- 1/4 papaya, sliced
- 1/2 orange, sliced
- 1/4 cup pear juice
- 1/2 teaspoon sliced ginger
- 1/4 cup ice cubes

DIRECTIONS

1. Place all of the ingredients in your blender, and blend for about 30 seconds, or until desired consistency is reached.

Nutritional Info: Calories: 104 | Sodium: 10mg | Dietary Fiber: 2.9g | Total Fat: 0.3g | Total Carbs: 17g | Protein: 0.9g.

Relax

SERVINGS: 1

This recipe won't put you to sleep, but it will help relieve some of the day's stress. The minerals and other nutrients in this smoothie will work on your muscles, skin and mind to give you a relaxing, more confident glow..

INGREDIENTS

- 3 ounces dried oatmeal
- 3 ounces finely chopped raw almonds
- 3/4 bananas
- 1 1/4 cups coconut water
- 1 tablespoon sweetener of your choice (honey is preferred)

DIRECTIONS

1. Place all of the ingredients in your blender, and blend for about 30 seconds, or until desired consistency is reached.

Nutritional Info: Calories: 545 | Sodium: 300mg | Dietary Fiber: 14g | Total Fat: 30.4g | Total Carbs: 60.1g | Protein: 17g.

Wake Up

This high energy-producing smoothie can fight those dark circles under your eyes. The ample sources of vitamin C, A, and Omega 3s in this recipe will leave you feeling refreshed and energized.

INGREDIENTS

- 1 tablespoons goji berries
- 1 cups raspberries
- 1 cups blueberries
- 1 1/2 tablespoons flaxseed powder (or ground flaxseed)
- 3 ounces low fat plain or vanilla yogurt
- 1 cup purified water or juice

DIRECTIONS

1. Place all of the ingredients in your blender, and blend for about 30 seconds, or until desired consistency is reached.

Nutritional Info: Calories: 377 | Sodium: 55mg | Dietary Fiber: 14.5g | Total Fat: 4.0g | Total Carbs: 52.7g | Protein: 7.5.

Wrinkle Be Gone

Yet another not very complex recipe which is extremely beneficial to your overall health and particularly your skin. These simple ingredients give your skin the nutrients it needs to become healthier and younger looking.

INGREDIENTS

- 1 cup blueberries
- 1 medium avocados, peeled and pitted
- 1 tablespoon flaxseed, ground
- 1 1/4 cups coconut water
- 1 tablespoon honey (or sweetener of choice)

DIRECTIONS

1. Place all of the ingredients in your blender, and blend for about 30 seconds, or until desired consistency is reached.

Nutritional Info: Calories: 288 | Sodium: 274mg | Dietary Fiber: 11.3g | Total Fat: 8.2g | Total Carbs: 52.9g | Protein: 5.3g.

CHAPTER 8
Bones & Joints

Osteo Punch

SERVINGS: 1

Your bones have never had it so good! Drink these on a regular basis and you'll not only feel stronger, but your bones and joints will be fortified.

INGREDIENTS

- 1/4 avocado
- 1/4 cup broccoli
- 2 tablespoons wheat bran
- 5 whole almonds, chopped
- 1/2 cup kale or spinach
- 3/4 cups spring water or almond milk

DIRECTIONS

1. Place all of the ingredients in your blender, and blend for about 30 seconds, or until desired consistency is reached.

Nutritional Info: Calories: 177 | Sodium: 25mg | Dietary Fiber: 8.3g | Total Fat: 13.2g | Total Carbs: 15.3g | Protein: 5g.

Strong Bones

This smoothie is especially loaded with calcium and antioxidants, which support bone and joint strength.

INGREDIENTS

- 1/4 banana
- 1/2 cup kale or romaine lettuce
- 1/4 cup blueberries
- 2 tablespoons wheat bran
- 8 whole cashews, chopped
- 3/4 cups spring water or milk of choice

DIRECTIONS

1. Place all of the ingredients in your blender, and blend for about 30 seconds, or until desired consistency is reached.

Nutritional Info: Calories: 239 | Sodium: 15mg | Dietary Fiber: 6.3g | Total Fat: 13.5g | Total Carbs: 29.2g | Protein: 7.7g.

CHAPTER 9
Constipation

Epsom Salt Surprise

This recipe will get your system working in a relatively short amount of time. The Epsom salts pull water into the colon, which in turn makes it much easier to go to the restroom. After this smoothie, you should probably hang around the house for a while. Good luck!

INGREDIENTS

- 1/4 cup applesauce
- 1/4 cup plain yogurt
- 1/2 tablespoon Epsom salt
- 1/4 cup spring water
- 1/4 banana
- 1/4 cup ice cubes
- 3 pitted prunes

DIRECTIONS

1. Place all of the ingredients in your blender, and blend for about 30 seconds, or until desired consistency is reached.

Nutritional Info: Calories: 136 | Sodium: 47mg | Dietary Fiber: 2.7g | Total Fat: 0.9g | Total Carbs: 28.7g | Protein: 4.3g.

Prune

This smoothie is designed to relieve constipation. Prunes and apples have a high fiber content, and can be quite flavorful.

INGREDIENTS

- 3 pitted prunes
- 1/2 cup ice cubes
- 1/2 cup plain yogurt
- 1/4 teaspoon cinnamon powder
- 1/2 cup apple juice
- 1 tablespoon honey (if desired for sweetness)

DIRECTIONS

1. Place all of the ingredients in your blender, and blend for about 30 seconds, or until desired consistency is reached.

Nutritional Info: Calories: 248 | Sodium: 50mg | Dietary Fiber: 4.5g | Total Fat: 1.9g | Total Carbs: 75g | Protein: 4.8g.

CHAPTER 10
Detox

Algae for Everyone

This smoothie contains so many beneficial elements that there just isn't room to mention them all. However, the blue-green algae that we've added to this highly nutritious drink is full of essential amino acids and is packed with protein.

INGREDIENTS

2 kale leaves, chopped
1/4 cup spinach, chopped
1 1/4 cups coconut water
1/4 cup parsley leaves (no stems)
1/4 cup cilantro
1 apple (green preferably)
1/4 ginger root, peeled and grated
1 tablespoon blue-green algae powder

DIRECTIONS

1. Place all of the ingredients in your blender, and blend for about 30 seconds, or until desired consistency is reached.

Nutritional Info: Calories: 181 | Sodium: 249mg | Dietary Fiber: 9g | Total Fat: 1g | Total Carbs: 43.6g | Protein: 3.9g.

Avo-Cucumber

This smoothie has a bit of everything in it. Try it, you'll love it.

INGREDIENTS

1/4 avocado

1/4 cucumber

1/4 pear

1/8 lemon

1/8 cup cilantro

1/2-inch ginger, peeled and sliced

3/4 cups kale (tightly packed)

3 ounces coconut water

1/8 cup protein powder

1 cup water

DIRECTIONS

1. Place all of the ingredients in your blender, and blend for about 30 seconds, or until desired consistency is reached.

Nutritional Info: Calories: 192 | Sodium: 119mg | Dietary Fiber: 4.4g | Total Fat: 6.9g | Total Carbs: 20.4g | Protein: 8.6g.

Beet This

This is the perfect detox recipe. This beet smoothie has nutrients that will benefit your whole body, while beets especially target the liver. The high fiber content will also fill you up for hours at a time.

INGREDIENTS

1/2 medium sized beet, cleaned and sliced
1 apple, peeled, sliced, seeds and core removed
2.5 ounces parsley
1 tablespoon chia seeds
1/2-inch of ginger, peeled and sliced
3/4 lemons, peeled, sliced, seeds removed
1 cup kale leaves, chopped
8 ounces purified water

DIRECTIONS

1. Place all of the ingredients in your blender, and blend for about 30 seconds, or until desired consistency is reached.

Nutritional Info: Calories: 267 | Sodium: 40mg | Dietary Fiber: 13.2g | Total Fat: 4.2g | Total Carbs: 30.7g | Protein: 5.5g.

Berry Minty Apple

SERVINGS: 1

This tasty concoction will keep you full as it works to gently detoxify your system.

INGREDIENTS

- 1/4 cup mixed berries (frozen or fresh)
- 5 leaves of mint
- 1/2 apple, peeled, sliced, seeds removed
- 3 romaine lettuce leaves
- 10 ounces purified water (or juice, if desired)

DIRECTIONS

1. Place all of the ingredients in your blender, and blend for about 30 seconds, or until desired consistency is reached.

Nutritional Info: Calories: 80 | Sodium: 2mg | Dietary Fiber: 4.1g | Total Fat: 0.4g | Total Carbs: 18.1g | Protein: 0.6g.

Blue Ginger

This delicious, low calorie smoothie is packed with antioxidants, vitamins and minerals. Plus, the anti-inflammatory ginger is a great for fighting infections.

INGREDIENTS

- 1/4 cup blueberries
- 1 banana (fresh or frozen)
- 2 ice cubes
- 1/4 cup ginger juice
- 1 1/4 cups soy milk (or preferred milk)

DIRECTIONS

1. Place all of the ingredients in your blender, and blend for about 30 seconds, or until desired consistency is reached.

Nutritional Info: Calories: 286 | Sodium: 103mg | Dietary Fiber: 9.2g | Total Fat: 4.8g | Total Carbs: 54.6g | Protein: 10.4g.

Cilantro Detox

Cilantro is great for detoxing because it bonds with heavy metals in the body and helps to eliminate them and other toxins. Cilantro also helps in lowering LDL (or bad cholesterol) levels, which benefits heart health.

INGREDIENTS

- 1/4 avocado, sliced
- 1/8 lemon, peeled and seeded
- 1/4 pear
- 1/8 cucumber, peeled and sliced
- 1/2 cup kale (or romaine lettuce)
- 1/4-ounce sliced ginger
- 1.5 ounces protein powder (hemp or pea)
- 1 1/2 tablespoons cilantro, chopped

DIRECTIONS

1. Place all of the ingredients in your blender, and blend for about 30 seconds, or until desired consistency is reached.

Nutritional Info: Calories: 232 | Sodium: 52mg | Dietary Fiber: 4.1g | Total Fat: 6.4g | Total Carbs: 14.5g | Protein: 15.2g.

Cranberry, Cranberry

Cranberries are terrific for detoxing the kidneys, and they're delicious. Studies have also shown that cranberries can effectively fight urinary tract infections in men and women.

INGREDIENTS

    1 cup purified water or cranberry juice
    3 ounces cranberries
    1/2 cucumber, peeled and sliced
    1/2 celery stalk, sliced
    3/4 apples, peeled, cored and seeds removed
    3/4 pears, cored and sliced
    1/4 cup spinach

DIRECTIONS

1. Place all of the ingredients in your blender, and blend for about 30 seconds, or until desired consistency is reached.

Nutritional Info: Calories: 200 | Sodium: 15mg | Dietary Fiber: 12g | Total Fat: 0.4g | Total Carbs: 47g | Protein: 1.1g.

Cucumber Kale

Cilantro is a great natural detoxifier. Spinach and kale, besides being super nutritious, are great cleansers as well. Toxins bind to these greens and are more easily eliminated from the body.

INGREDIENTS

1/4 cucumber, sliced
1/2 cup kale (or romaine lettuce or spinach)
3/4 cups spring water
8 teaspoons cilantro, chopped
1/4 lemon, peeled and seeded
1/2 wedge lime, peeled and seeded
1/4 cup cilantro

DIRECTIONS

1. Place all of the ingredients in your blender, and blend for about 30 seconds, or until desired consistency is reached.

Nutritional Info: Calories: 25 | Sodium: 10mg | Dietary Fiber: 1.7g | Total Fat: 0.1g | Total Carbs: 7.2g | Protein: 1g.

Detox Berry

SERVINGS: 1

This smoothie tastes great and clears the body of harmful toxins.

INGREDIENTS

- 1/3 cups frozen cherries, pitted
- 1/2 cup frozen raspberries
- 1/2 cup rice milk or almond milk
- 1 1/4 tablespoons honey
- 3/4 tablespoons ginger (finely grated)
- 1 tablespoon flaxseeds
- 1/2 tablespoon lemon juice

DIRECTIONS

1. Place all of the ingredients in your blender, and blend for about 30 seconds, or until desired consistency is reached.

Nutritional Info: Calories: 276 | Sodium: 25mg | Dietary Fiber: 3.5g | Total Fat: 1.2g | Total Carbs: 38.0g | Protein: 1.8g.

Feel Good

This drink is loaded with antioxidants and has plenty of vitamins and energy giving nutrients. The Goji berry is also a stress reliever, and has been shown to enhance feelings of wellbeing.

INGREDIENTS

- 3/4 cups blueberries
- 3/4 cups coconut milk
- 6 tablespoons blackberries
- 6 tablespoons raspberries
- 1/2 cup Goji berries (these should soak for 10-15 minutes before blending)
- 1 tablespoon flaxseed, ground
- 2 dates, pitted
- 1 cup purified water

DIRECTIONS

1. Place all of the ingredients in your blender, and blend for about 30 seconds, or until desired consistency is reached.

Nutritional Info: Calories: 325 | Sodium: 35mg | Dietary Fiber: 13.7g | Total Fat: 23.5g | Total Carbs: 32.0g | Protein: 4.8g.

Fiberlicious

There's plenty of fiber in this one; it will keep you full and help maintain regular bowel movements.

INGREDIENTS

- 1 cup almond milk or soymilk
- 1/4 avocado
- 1/2 pear, sliced
- 3/4 cups spinach (tightly packed)
- 1/4 cup coconut water
- 1/2 tablespoon chia seeds
- 1/4 cup protein powder
- 1 1/2 cups water

DIRECTIONS

1. Place all of the ingredients in your blender, and blend for about 30 seconds, or until desired consistency is reached.

Nutritional Info: Calories: 450 | Sodium: 98mg | Dietary Fiber: 8.5g | Total Fat: 35.0g | Total Carbs: 23.5g | Protein: 13.5g.

Goji Goodness

SERVINGS: 1

This delightful drink will not only tickle your palate, but it will also help rid toxins from your system while giving you a sense of wellbeing.

INGREDIENTS

1 banana
1/4 cup strawberries (frozen or fresh)
1/4 cup Goji berries
1 1/4 cups coconut water
2 ice cubes

DIRECTIONS

1. Place all of the ingredients in your blender, and blend for about 30 seconds, or until desired consistency is reached.

Nutritional Info: Calories: 115| Sodium: 136mg | Dietary Fiber: 4.6g | Total Fat: 0.8g | Total Carbs: 26.0g | Protein: 3.0g.

Jicama Surprise

The surprise is that it tastes so good. This recipe also provides plenty of vitamin C and fiber.

INGREDIENTS

1/2 lime
1/2 cucumber, chopped
1/2 apple, chopped
5 romaine leaves
1/2 avocado, sliced
1/2 cup jicama (grated or sliced)
1/4 cup cilantro
1/4 cup protein powder
2 pitted dates
1 1/4 cups water

DIRECTIONS

1. Place all of the ingredients in your blender, and blend for about 30 seconds, or until desired consistency is reached.

Nutritional Info: Calories: 210 | Sodium: 43mg | Dietary Fiber: 8.0g | Total Fat: 12.0g | Total Carbs: 26.0g | Protein: 12.3g.

Kale/Mango Detox

This is one of the easier detox smoothies to make. Besides being uniquely delicious, the ingredients make this smoothie high in fiber, iron, antioxidants, vitamins A, C, K and Calcium.

INGREDIENTS

- 3/4 cups orange juice
- 1/8 cup chopped parsley
- 3/4 chopped celery stems
- 3/4 cups cubed mango
- 3/4 cups chopped kale leaves

DIRECTIONS

1. Place all of the ingredients in your blender, and blend for about 30 seconds, or until desired consistency is reached.

Nutritional Info: Calories: 87 | Sodium: 24mg | Dietary Fiber: 1.3g | Total Fat: 0.3g | Total Carbs: 18.1g | Protein: 1.3g.

Smooth As Silk

This recipe works inside and out. It aids in alleviating toxins, while also working to clarify and rejuvenate your complexion.

INGREDIENTS

- 1 apple, peeled, cored, seeded
- 3/4 limes, peeled, sliced, seeded
- 6 tablespoons parsley (leaves only, no stems)
- 1 tablespoons coconut oil
- 1 1/2 tablespoons leaves of mint
- 1/2 large cucumber, peeled and sliced
- 1/2 cup coconut water
- 1 cup purified water or juice

DIRECTIONS

1. Place all of the ingredients in your blender, and blend for about 30 seconds, or until desired consistency is reached.

Nutritional Info: Calories: 210 | Sodium: 90mg | Dietary Fiber: 4.1g | Total Fat: 7.3g | Total Carbs: 38.4g | Protein: 1.9g.

Spicy Carrot

This smoothie will make your hair stand up straight. Depending, of course, on how much jalapeno you add to it. Either way, this bold drink is designed to maintain a healthy heart.

INGREDIENTS

- 1 - 2 tomatoes
- 2.5 carrots
- 1 bell peppers, sliced and seeded (preferably red)
- 1.5 garlic cloves
- 1 1/2 celery stalks, chopped
- 1/2 cup spinach
- 1/2 red jalapeno, seeded
- 1/4 cup watercress

DIRECTIONS

1. Place all of the ingredients in your blender, and blend for about 30 seconds, or until desired consistency is reached.

Nutritional Info: Calories: 85 | Sodium: 190mg | Dietary Fiber: 4.3g | Total Fat: 0.4g | Total Carbs: 16.4g | Protein: 2.2g.

Spirulina Special Source

SERVINGS: 1

The Aztecs used to carry spirulina with them when they went on long trips. It not only gave them nourishment, but it also helped them detox.

INGREDIENTS

- 1/2 banana
- 1/4 avocado
- 1/2 cup almond milk or soymilk
- 1/2 cup blueberries
- 1/2 tablespoon spirulina powder
- 1/4 cup protein powder
- 1 cup water

DIRECTIONS

1. Place all of the ingredients in your blender, and blend for about 30 seconds, or until desired consistency is reached.

Nutritional Info: Calories: 209 | Sodium: 75mg | Dietary Fiber: 5.3g | Total Fat: 20.4g | Total Carbs: 19.1g | Protein: 9.1g.

Super Cleanse

SERVINGS: 1

Parsley and celery are diuretics and help the body get rid of toxins. Kale and mangos enhance detoxification because of their superfood nutrients.

INGREDIENTS

- 1/2 cup kale (or romaine lettuce)
- 1/2 cup orange juice
- 1/4 cup mango, sliced
- 1/8 cup parsley, chopped
- 1/2 stalk celery, chopped

DIRECTIONS

1. Place all of the ingredients in your blender, and blend for about 30 seconds, or until desired consistency is reached.

Nutritional Info: Calories: 67 | Sodium: 18mg | Dietary Fiber: 1.6g | Total Fat: 0.3g | Total Carbs: 18.4g | Protein: 2.6g.

Sweet Fruit Detox Special

SERVINGS: 1

This smoothie is sweet and powerful. You'll love the taste and what it does for your health.

INGREDIENTS

- 3/4 tablespoons lemon zest
- 1 1/4 cups strawberries (fresh or frozen)
- 1 3/4 cups non-dairy milk of choice
- 1/2 orange, peeled
- 3/4 bananas
- 1 cup spinach

DIRECTIONS

1. Place all of the ingredients in your blender, and blend for about 30 seconds, or until desired consistency is reached.

Nutritional Info: Calories: 182 | Sodium: 126mg | Dietary Fiber: 11.2g | Total Fat: 4.3g | Total Carbs: 33.5g | Protein: 9.4g.

Tangy Blueberry

SERVINGS: 1

This simple smoothly contains an extraordinary amount of B vitamins, along with vitamin C, K, E, and minerals such as iron, calcium, manganese and copper. It also helps in the fight against infections because of its antioxidant properties.

INGREDIENTS

- 1/4 cup blueberries
- 1 lemon, peeled, sliced and seeded
- 1 tablespoon honey (or sweetener of choice)
- 1 1/4 cups purified water

DIRECTIONS

1. Place all of the ingredients in your blender, and blend for about 30 seconds, or until desired consistency is reached.

Nutritional Info: Calories: 18 | Sodium: 0.5mg | Dietary Fiber: 1.5g | Total Fat: 0.0g | Total Carbs: 12.3g | Protein: 0.5g.

Zesty Apple

This smoothie is perfect for reducing inflammation, and gently works on detoxing your system.

INGREDIENTS

3/4 lemons, peeled, sliced and seeded
1 apple (green preferably)
1/2 cucumber, peeled and sliced
3 leaves of red lettuce
1/4 cup mango cubes (frozen or fresh)
1 teaspoons barley grass powder
8 ounces purified water

DIRECTIONS

1. Place all of the ingredients in your blender, and blend for about 30 seconds, or until desired consistency is reached.

Nutritional Info: Calories: 94 | Sodium: 9mg | Dietary Fiber: 3.7g | Total Fat: 0.4g | Total Carbs: 24.0g | Protein: 1.4g.

CHAPTER 11
Blood Sugar

Kale-Apple

This smoothie will brighten your day, give you plenty of energy, and keep your blood sugar stable.

INGREDIENTS

- 1 cup kale or spinach
- 1/4 cup Greek yogurt
- 1/4 cup apple or orange juice (unsweetened)
- 3 teaspoons flaxseeds
- 1 teaspoon maple syrup
- 1/2 cup ice cubes

DIRECTIONS

1. Place all of the ingredients in your blender, and blend for about 30 seconds, or until desired consistency is reached.

Nutritional Info: Calories: 79 | Sodium: 39mg | Dietary Fiber: 2.3g | Total Fat: 1.4g | Total Carbs: 12.4g | Protein: 7.3g.

Zesty Lime

This is a delicious and nutritious smoothie, also good for people with have Type 2 diabetes.

INGREDIENTS

- 1/4 cup lime juice
- 1/2 cup almond milk
- 1/2 banana (frozen)
- 3/4 cups kale (or spinach)
- 3 ice cubes
- 1 tablespoon almond butter (or sunflower butter)
- 1 pitted dates

DIRECTIONS

1. Place all of the ingredients in your blender, and blend for about 30 seconds, or until desired consistency is reached.

Nutritional Info: Calories: 243 | Sodium: 30mg | Dietary Fiber: 3.1g | Total Fat: 18.2g | Total Carbs: 16.2g | Protein: 4.3g.

CHAPTER 12
Immune System

Avocado

Avocados are packed with nutrients that maintain a healthy immune system. These fruits are full of zinc, selenium, folic acid, iron and vitamins B6, E, A and C. Avocados are a true superfood.

INGREDIENTS

1/4 avocado
1/4 banana
1 tablespoon honey
1 /2cup ice cubes
1/4 cup spring water
8 teaspoons lime juice
1/2 tablespoon chai seeds
1/4 mango (peeled, pitted and cubed)

DIRECTIONS

1. Place all of the ingredients in your blender, and blend for about 30 seconds, or until desired consistency is reached.

Nutritional Info: Calories: 105 | Sodium: 4.5mg | Dietary Fiber: 3.2g | Total Fat: 6.1g | Total Carbs: 15.0g | Protein: 1.2g.

Granny Green

SERVINGS: 1

Ginger is a natural anti-inflammatory food and a strong infection-fighter. All the elements in this smoothie have a synergistic effect on your immune system. When combined, they work even more effectively to strengthen your system and keep you healthy.

INGREDIENTS

- 1/2 Granny Smith apple, sliced and seeded
- 1/4 pear
- 1/2 celery stalk, chopped
- 1/2 cup kale
- 1/2 tablespoon ginger
- 1/2 cup ice cubes
- 1/4 cup spring water or apple juice

DIRECTIONS

1. Place all of the ingredients in your blender, and blend for about 30 seconds, or until desired consistency is reached.

Nutritional Info: Calories: 75 | Sodium: 14mg | Dietary Fiber: 2.1g | Total Fat: 0.2g | Total Carbs: 15.7g | Protein: 0.8g.

he Cold Fighter

is smoothie will not only energize you, but will also satisfy your hunger pangs and help fight f those nasty colds in the winter.

GREDIENTS

- 1/2 carrot
- 1/4 beet, chopped
- 1/2 celery stalk, chopped
- 1/4 cucumber, peeled and sliced
- 1/2 tablespoon of ginger, peeled and sliced
- 1/2 cup ice cubes
- 1/4 cup spring water

RECTIONS

1. Place all of the ingredients in your blender, and blend for about 30 seconds, or until desired consistency is reached.

utritional Info: Calories: 23 | Sodium: 26mg | Dietary Fiber: 1.1g | Total Fat: 0.1g | tal Carbs: 5.4g | Protein: 0.76g.

CHAPTER 13
Beauty

Romantic Veggie

This smoothie has a creamy texture, and the delicious tang of veggies. What you will really appreciate is its ability to relax your muscles and lower blood pressure, giving you a youthful glow.

INGREDIENTS

- 1/2 medium tomato
- 1/4 red bell pepper, sliced
- 1 cloves garlic
- 1/2 celery stalk
- 1/2 carrot, sliced
- 1/2 cup kale (or romaine lettuce)
- 1/2 cup ice cubes

DIRECTIONS

1. Place all of the ingredients in your blender, and blend for about 30 seconds, or until desired consistency is reached.

Nutritional Info: Calories: 27 | Sodium: 26mg | Dietary Fiber: 1.4g | Total Fat: 0.1g | Total Carbs: 6.4g | Protein: 1.1g.

Royal Avocado

SERVINGS: 1

Silky skin is attainable with these wonderful ingredients. The avocado is a marvelous food for great skin and hair, and the synergistic effect it has when combined with these other ingredients is incredible.

INGREDIENTS

1/4 avocado (ripe) OR 4 tablespoons almond butter
1/4 cucumber
1/2 cup kale or Bok Choy or romaine lettuce
1/4 banana
6 tablespoons blueberries
1/2 cup spring water or coconut water

DIRECTIONS

1. We don't recommend a sweetener for this, but if you must, you must. Go lightly and use honey if necessary.
2. Place all of the ingredients in your blender, and blend for about 30 seconds, or until desired consistency is reached.

Nutritional Info: Calories: 47 | Sodium: 9mg | Dietary Fiber: 1.5g | Total Fat: 0.4g | Total Carbs: 10.1g | Protein: 1.2g.

CHAPTER 14
Energy-Boost

Berry Burst

This excellent smoothie will give you a burst of energy that will last a long time. The soy milk and flaxseeds give this berry smoothie a stabilizing effect, so you won't feel your energy crash like you might after eating a chocolate bar.

INGREDIENTS

- 1/2 cup almond or soy milk
- 1/4 cup blackberries
- 1/4 cup blueberries
- 1/2 banana (frozen)
- 1/2 tablespoon honey
- 3/4 tablespoons flaxseed
- 1/4 cup ice cubes

DIRECTIONS

1. Place all of the ingredients in your blender, and blend for about 30 seconds, or until desired consistency is reached.

Nutritional Info: Calories: 210 | Sodium: 3mg | Dietary Fiber: 6.1g | Total Fat: 13g | Total Carbs: 21.2g | Protein: 6.2g.

Green Goblin

After blending, chill in the refrigerator, then blend briskly again right before serving. This smoothie will give you lots of energy. Your competitors will wonder how you stay so far ahead of them all the time. Let them keep wondering. It's good for them.

INGREDIENTS

- 1/2 cup kale or spinach, chopped
- 1/2 apple, peeled, sliced, seeded
- 1/4 cup green seedless grapes
- 1/2 kiwi, sliced and peeled
- 1/2 cup honeydew melon, chopped and peeled

DIRECTIONS

1. Place all of the ingredients in your blender, and blend for about 30 seconds, or until desired consistency is reached.

Nutritional Info: Calories: 82 | Sodium: 15mg | Dietary Fiber: 2.4g | Total Fat: 0.3g | Total Carbs: 16.2g | Protein: 1.3g.

Mean Green Machine

SERVINGS: 1

This one is a winner. You can drink this smoothie before or after a workout and feel great. It pumps a lot of nutrition your way and delivers plenty of protein and flavor.

INGREDIENTS

- 1/2 cup of kale or spinach, chopped
- 1/2 stalk of celery, chopped
- 1/2 apple, sliced
- 1/2 tablespoon lemon juice
- 1/6 or 33 g cucumber, sliced
- 1/2 cup ice cubes
- 1/8 cup spring water

DIRECTIONS

1. Place all of the ingredients in your blender, and blend for about 30 seconds, or until desired consistency is reached.

Nutritional Info: Calories: 31 | Sodium: 13mg | Dietary Fiber: 1.5g | Total Fat: 0.2g | Total Carbs: 7.8g | Protein: 0.6g.

CHAPTER 15
Health

Apple Caramel

Sounds good, but tastes even better—and it's good for you.

INGREDIENTS

- 1/8 cup caramel sauce
- 1/2 cup low fat vanilla yogurt
- 1 cups apple juice
- 1/2 tablespoon cinnamon
- 1 tablespoons sweetener of choice
- 3 ice cubes

DIRECTIONS

1. Place all of the ingredients in your blender, and blend for about 30 seconds, or until desired consistency is reached.

Nutritional Info: Calories: 157 | Sodium: 120mg | Dietary Fiber: 1.8g | Total Fat: 0.6g | Total Carbs: 37.3g | Protein: 2.0g.

Delicious Banana Cream

This low-calorie dessert smoothie lives up to its name and provides lots of nutrients and energy.

INGREDIENTS

- 1/2 cup low fat vanilla yogurt
- 3/4 banana
- 1 cup vanilla almond milk
- 1/4 cup low fat cottage cheese
- 1/8 cup cream cheese (low fat)
- 1/4 teaspoon cinnamon

DIRECTIONS

1. Place all of the ingredients in your blender, and blend for about 30 seconds, or until desired consistency is reached.

Nutritional Info: Calories: 199 | Sodium: 258.2mg | Dietary Fiber: 1.9g | Total Fat: 7.8g | Total Carbs: 27.0g | Protein: 7.9g.

Banana Pumpkin

Banana and pumpkin are great anytime of the year and even better together—nutritionally and taste-wise.

INGREDIENTS

- 3/4 cups soymilk or low fat milk
- 3 kale leaves
- 1 tablespoons flaxseed oil
- 3/4 bananas
- 1/4 teaspoon cinnamon
- 1/2 cup pumpkin puree (fresh or canned)
- 3 ice cubes

DIRECTIONS

1. Place all of the ingredients in your blender, and blend for about 30 seconds, or until desired consistency is reached.

Nutritional Info: Calories: 230 | Sodium: 105mg | Dietary Fiber: 5.2g | Total Fat: 8.1g | Total Carbs: 32.5g | Protein: 7.3g.

Berry Carrot

This great tasting smoothie lets you drink your way to better health.

INGREDIENTS

- 1/2 cup frozen berries (your choice or mixed)
- 1/2 cup low fat milk or almond milk
- 1 cups juice or water
- 3/4 carrots
- 1 tablespoon chia seeds
- 1/8 cup protein powder

DIRECTIONS

1. Place all of the ingredients in your blender, and blend for about 30 seconds, or until desired consistency is reached.

Nutritional Info: Calories: 210 | Sodium: 127mg | Dietary Fiber: 2.5g | Total Fat: 2.3g | Total Carbs: 36.2g | Protein: 13g.

Berry-Granate

When you mix pomegranate and berries together you get a high energy drink that's filled with antioxidants.

INGREDIENTS

- 1 cup silken tofu
- 1 cup pomegranate juice
- 1 1/2 cups mixed berries (fresh or frozen)
- 1/8 cup honey or sweetener of your choice

DIRECTIONS

1. Place all of the ingredients in your blender, and blend for about 30 seconds, or until desired consistency is reached.

Nutritional Info: Calories: 226 | Sodium: 21mg | Dietary Fiber: 3.9g | Total Fat: 1.5g | Total Carbs: 48.8g | Protein: 3.7g.

Cafe Banana

SERVINGS: 1

Add a superfood to coffee and you get a wonderful and filling wake up smoothie.

INGREDIENTS

3/4 bananas
1 cups coffee (cold)
1/4 cup protein powder
1/4 cup low fat milk or soymilk
1/4 cup dry oats

DIRECTIONS

1. Place all of the ingredients in your blender, and blend for about 30 seconds, or until desired consistency is reached.

Nutritional Info: Calories: 122 | Sodium: 47mg | Dietary Fiber: 2.2g | Total Fat: 1.5g | Total Carbs: 19.9g | Protein: 8.1g.

Chocolate Divine

SERVINGS: 1

This creamy smoothie is not only divinely delicious, but it also has elements that make it a nutritious drink.

INGREDIENTS

1/8 cup cocoa powder or chocolate syrup

1/4 cup coconut milk

3 dates (pitted)

1 cup low fat milk or soymilk

1 tablespoon sweetener of choice

3 ice cubes

DIRECTIONS

1. Place all of the ingredients in your blender, and blend for about 30 seconds, or until desired consistency is reached.

Nutritional Info: Calories: 167.5 | Sodium: 70mg | Dietary Fiber: 4.3g | Total Fat: 9,1g | Total Carbs: 21.4g | Protein: 12.1g.

Chocolatey Date

Antioxidants and a great deal of high energy elements are provided by this great smoothie.

INGREDIENTS

1/2 cup pitted dates
1/4 cup almonds
1/4 cup cocoa or chocolate syrup
1 cup boiling water
1/2 cup silken tofu
3 ice cubes

DIRECTIONS

1. Add the ice and tofu after you've let the other ingredients sit in the boiling water in the blender for 10 minutes. This will soften them up for the blending phase.
2. Blend for about 30 seconds, or until desired consistency is reached.

Nutritional Info: Calories: 231 | Sodium: 25mg | Dietary Fiber: 8.25g | Total Fat: 8.1g | Total Carbs: 42.3g | Protein: 7.0g.

Coconut Almond

SERVINGS: 1

This smoothie is high in immune protecting nutrients and packs a great deal of protein and vitamin C.

INGREDIENTS

- 3/4 cups coconut water
- 3/4 cups almond milk
- 1 tablespoons honey (or sweetener of choice)
- 1/2 cup cubed pineapple (fresh or frozen)
- 1/8 cup shredded coconut
- 1/4 teaspoon vanilla extract

DIRECTIONS

1. Place all of the ingredients in your blender, and blend for about 30 seconds, or until desired consistency is reached.

Nutritional Info: Calories: 296 | Sodium: 110mg | Dietary Fiber: 4.0g | Total Fat: 23.4g | Total Carbs: 23.2g | Protein: 3.2g.

Flaxseed Spinach

SERVINGS: 1

This smoothie is protein rich and has a lot of fiber and plenty of Omega-3s, all of which promote and support optimal health.

INGREDIENTS

- 3/4 bananas
- 3 strawberries (frozen or fresh)
- 1/2 tablespoon flaxseed oil
- 1/8 cup peanut butter
- 3/4 cups low fat milk or soymilk
- 1/2 cup low fat plain or vanilla yogurt

DIRECTIONS

1. Place all of the ingredients in your blender, and blend for about 30 seconds, or until desired consistency is reached.

Nutritional Info: Calories: 257 | Sodium: 141mg | Dietary Fiber: 2.5g | Total Fat: 13.2g | Total Carbs: 28.8g | Protein: 8.2g.

Green Tea Banana

Green tea is a great way to burn fat and stay healthy; it's also a terrific way to wake up in the morning.

INGREDIENTS

- 3/4 bananas
- 1/2 honeydew melon (scooped in pieces away from rind)
- 3/4 cups brewed green tea
- 1 tablespoons honey or sweetener of your choice
- 1/4 cup low fat milk or soy or almond milk

DIRECTIONS

1. Place all of the ingredients in your blender, and blend for about 30 seconds, or until desired consistency is reached.

Nutritional Info: Calories: 226 | Sodium: 78.9mg | Dietary Fiber: 3.9g | Total Fat: 0.9g | Total Carbs: 63g | Protein: 3.4g.

KC Delight (Kale/Coconut)

SERVINGS: 1

When you combine a superfood like kale with a miracle food like coconut, you get a healthy and extremely delicious smoothie.

INGREDIENTS

- 3/4 bananas
- 1 cup chopped kale
- 1 tablespoon flaxseed oil
- 1/8 cup honey or sweetener (your choice)
- 1/4 teaspoon coconut extract
- 3 ice cubes

DIRECTIONS

1. Place all of the ingredients in your blender, and blend for about 30 seconds, or until desired consistency is reached.

Nutritional Info: Calories: 188 | Sodium: 27mg | Dietary Fiber: 1.7g | Total Fat: 7.15g | Total Carbs: 31.3g | Protein: 1.6g.

Lemon Strawberry

SERVINGS: 1

This smoothie is not only refreshing, but also full of vitamin C and other health supporting nutrients.

INGREDIENTS

   1/2 cup strawberries (fresh or frozen)
   1 cup low fat milk or soymilk
   5 almonds, raw
   1/8 cup lemon juice
   1/2 teaspoon lemon zest
   3 ice cubes

DIRECTIONS

1.   Place all of the ingredients in your blender, and blend for about 30 seconds, or until desired consistency is reached.

Nutritional Info: Calories: 84 | Sodium: 68mg | Dietary Fiber: 1.2 | Total Fat: 2.9 | Total Carbs: 10.1 | Protein: 5.2g.

Minty Spinach

Vitamin and mineral rich spinach combined with minty chocolate is hard to beat.

INGREDIENTS

- 1 cup low fat milk or almond milk
- 1/4 cup chocolate protein powder
- 1 cup frozen spinach (or 3 cups fresh spinach)
- 1/4 cup dry oats
- 1/8 teaspoon peppermint extract

DIRECTIONS

1. Place all of the ingredients in your blender, and blend for about 30 seconds, or until desired consistency is reached.

Nutritional Info: Calories: 125 | Sodium: 67mg | Dietary Fiber: 1.4g | Total Fat: 2.5g | Total Carbs: 14.3g | Protein: 11.2g.

PB&J

Now you can get all the eating enjoyment of your youth plus even more nutrition and energy, by drinking it.

INGREDIENTS

- 1/8 cup peanut butter
- 1/8 cup jam (flavor of choice)
- 3 ice cubes
- 1/4 teaspoon vanilla extract
- 1 1/4 cups low fat milk or soymilk
- 1/8 cup low fat plain or vanilla yogurt

DIRECTIONS

1. Place all of the ingredients in your blender, and blend for about 30 seconds, or until desired consistency is reached.

Nutritional Info: Calories: 259 | Sodium: 185mg | Dietary Fiber: 1.2g | Total Fat: 10.0g | Total Carbs: 32.9g | Protein: 10.8g.

Raisin Bliss

SERVINGS: 1

This smoothie provides long-lasting energy for a busy lifestyle.

INGREDIENTS

- 1 banana
- 1/4 cup protein powder (chocolate flavor is recommended)
- 1 teaspoons cinnamon
- 1/2 cup low fat vanilla or plain yogurt
- 1/2 tablespoon honey (or sweetener of choice)
- 3/4 cups low fat milk or soymilk
- 1/8 cup raisins
- 3 ice cubes

DIRECTIONS

1. Place all of the ingredients in your blender, and blend for about 30 seconds, or until desired consistency is reached.

Nutritional Info: Calories: 210 | Sodium: 126mg | Dietary Fiber: 2.5g | Total Fat: 2.3g | Total Carbs: 36g | Protein: 12.8g.

Smoothie Sundae

Instead of ice cream, try this low-calorie smoothie for increased energy and equally great flavor.

INGREDIENTS

- 1/2 cup low fat vanilla yogurt
- 3/4 cups low fat chocolate milk or chocolate soymilk
- 3/4 cups strawberries (fresh or frozen)
- 1 teaspoons flaxseed (ground)
- 1/4 cup chocolate or vanilla protein powder

DIRECTIONS

1. Place all of the ingredients in your blender, and blend for about 30 seconds, or until desired consistency is reached.

Nutritional Info: Calories: 212 | Sodium: 128mg | Dietary Fiber: 2.5g | Total Fat: 7.3g | Total Carbs: 30.1g | Protein: 6.7g.

Spunky Monkey

The three ingredients we loved as kids: chocolate, banana and peanut butter are back.

INGREDIENTS

3/4 bananas
1/8 cup peanut butter
1 cup low fat chocolate milk or chocolate soymilk
3 ice cubes
1 1/2 tablespoons sweetener (your choice)

DIRECTIONS

1. Place all of the ingredients in your blender, and blend for about 30 seconds, or until desired consistency is reached.

Nutritional Info: Calories: 179 | Sodium: 197mg | Dietary Fiber: 3.5g | Total Fat: 8.5g | Total Carbs: 21.5g | Protein: 8.5g.

Strawberry Peach

SERVINGS: 1

This summer favorite is tasty and keeps you satisfied for hours.

INGREDIENTS

- 3/4 bananas
- 3/4 cups strawberries (frozen or fresh)
- 1 cup low fat milk or soymilk
- 1/8 cup chia seeds
- 1 tablespoon honey (or sweetener of choice)

DIRECTIONS

1. Place all of the ingredients in your blender, and blend for about 30 seconds, or until desired consistency is reached.

Nutritional Info: Calories: 350 | Sodium: 55mg | Dietary Fiber: 2.9g | Total Fat: 2.2g | Total Carbs: 30.1g | Protein: 5.4g.

Veggie Spice

This smoothie has some heat, and provides a great source of energy.

INGREDIENTS

- 1/2 cup avocado
- 1/8 cup lemon juice
- 7 ounces carrot juice
- Dash of cayenne pepper
- 3/4 tablespoons fresh ginger (grated)
- 3 ice cubes

DIRECTIONS

1. Place all of the ingredients in your blender, and blend for about 30 seconds, or until desired consistency is reached.

Nutritional Info: Calories: 126 | Sodium: 85mg | Dietary Fiber: 5.2g | Total Fat: 7.4g | Total Carbs: 15g | Protein: 1.8g.

Melonberry

Combine watermelon with strawberry and you get this wonderful explosion of flavor, nutrition and energy.

INGREDIENTS

- 1/4 cup low fat milk or soymilk
- 1/2 medium-sized seedless watermelon (scooped out in cubes from rind)
- 1/2 cup strawberries (frozen or fresh)
- 1/2 cup low fat yogurt
- 1/8 cup protein powder
- 3 ice cubes

DIRECTIONS

1. Place all of the ingredients in your blender, and blend for about 30 seconds, or until desired consistency is reached.

Nutritional Info: Calories: 110 | Sodium: 98mg | Dietary Fiber: 0.9g | Total Fat: 1.7g | Total Carbs: 13.0g | Protein: 10.2g.

CHAPTER 16
Heart

Flaxseed Supreme

SERVINGS: 1

Flaxseeds are rich in Omega-3, which is an anti-inflammatory fatty acid that supports heart health. Antioxidants, along with minerals and vitamins from the other ingredients, strengthen the body and the heart against disease and infections.

INGREDIENTS

- 1/2 banana
- 1/4 orange (sliced)
- 1/4 cup berries (your choice)
- 1/4 avocado
- 3/4 cups kale or romaine lettuce
- 1/2 tablespoon flaxseeds (ground)
- 1/2 cup spring water

DIRECTIONS

1. Place all of the ingredients in your blender, and blend for about 30 seconds, or until desired consistency is reached.

Nutritional Info: Calories: 120 | Sodium: 13mg | Dietary Fiber: 4.4g | Total Fat: 5.6g | Total Carbs: 16.9g | Protein: 2.2g.

Hardy Heart

SERVINGS: 1

This smoothie is full of fiber, which removes toxins from your intestines and lowers your blood cholesterol. The greens in this tasty treat are also good for maintaining a healthy heart.

INGREDIENTS

- 1/2 cup cucumber, peeled and sliced
- 1/2 cup kale or spinach
- 1/2 celery stalk, chopped
- 1/4 cup parsley, chopped
- 1/2 tablespoon psyllium husks (or Metamucil)
- 1/2 apple, peeled and de-seeded
- 1 tablespoon lemon juice
- 1/2 tablespoon lime juice

DIRECTIONS

1. Place all of the ingredients in your blender, and blend for about 30 seconds, or until desired consistency is reached.

Nutritional Info: Calories: 65 | Sodium: 39mg | Dietary Fiber: 8.9g | Total Fat: 0.3g | Total Carbs: 19.1g | Protein: 1.2g.

Pomegranate Pump

SERVINGS: 1

This smoothie is full of antioxidants, and can help unclog your arteries.

INGREDIENTS

  1/4 banana
  3 strawberries
  1/2 cup plain yogurt
  1/2 cup pomegranate juice
  1/4 cup ice cubes

DIRECTIONS

1. Place all of the ingredients in your blender, and blend for about 30 seconds, or until desired consistency is reached.

Nutritional Info: Calories: 100 | Sodium: 47mg | Dietary Fiber: 0.8g | Total Fat: 0.8g | Total Carbs: 18.2g | Protein: 3.8g.

CHAPTER 17
Mood

Good Mood Oatmeal

SERVINGS: 1

Oatmeal helps to level out blood sugar levels and contains lots of fiber, which helps eliminate toxins in the intestines. Walnuts are also full of Omega-3s, which are healthy for your brain cells and lift your mood.

INGREDIENTS

- 1/8 cup rolled oats
- 1/2 cup plain yogurt
- 1/4 cup blackberries or blueberries
- 1/8 cup walnuts, chopped
- 1/2 tablespoon walnut oil
- 1/4 cup soy milk
- 1/4 cup spring water

DIRECTIONS

1. Place all of the ingredients in your blender, and blend for about 30 seconds, or until desired consistency is reached.

Nutritional Info: Calories: 148 | Sodium: 60mg | Dietary Fiber: 2.3g | Total Fat: 7.5g | Total Carbs: 12.4g | Protein: 7.8g.

Happy Green

SERVINGS: 1

Some people have told us that this smoothie has changed their mood for the better within minutes. Eating certain nutrients has been shown to increase feelings of wellness because of healthy vitamins and minerals that improve brain function. Flaxseed, for example, has been shown to help alleviate depression when taken on a regular basis.

INGREDIENTS

- 1/2 cup kale or spinach
- 1/8 cup Greek yogurt
- 1/2 cup soy or almond milk
- 1/2 tablespoon flaxseed, ground
- 1 1/2 tablespoons honey
- 1/2 banana (frozen if possible)
- 1/8 cup blueberries or blackberries
- 1/4 cup ice cubes

DIRECTIONS

1. Place all of the ingredients in your blender, and blend for about 30 seconds, or until desired consistency is reached.

Nutritional Info: Calories: 264 | Sodium: 38mg | Dietary Fiber: 3.0g | Total Fat: 15.0g | Total Carbs: 28.7g | Protein: 7.9g.

Up, Up and Away

SERVINGS: 1

This smoothie is a great mood enhancer. Swiss chard has a lot of magnesium, which can increase energy levels and improve emotional state.

INGREDIENTS

- 1/2 banana
- 1/2 teaspoon ginger (sliced)
- 1/2 cup Swiss chard
- 1/4 cup blueberries
- 1/2 cup spring water or coconut water
- 1/4 cup ice

DIRECTIONS

1. Place all of the ingredients in your blender, and blend for about 30 seconds, or until desired consistency is reached.

Nutritional Info: Calories: 40 | Sodium: 20mg | Dietary Fiber: 1.4g | Total Fat: 0.2g | Total Carbs: 10.0g | Protein: 0.7g.

CHAPTER 18
Performance

Oatmeal

Oatmeal is nourishing and fills you up for hours. We've added strawberries, bananas and milk for extra protein, antioxidants and potassium. This will keep any athlete energized for several hours.

INGREDIENTS

1/4 cup rolled oats
1/2 cup milk (soy or almond is okay too)
1/2 banana
1/4 cup strawberries

DIRECTIONS

1. Add sweetener if desired.
2. Place all of the ingredients in your blender, and blend for about 30 seconds, or until desired consistency is reached.

Nutritional Info: Calories: 102 | Sodium: 30mg | Dietary Fiber: 2.2g | Total Fat: 2.1g | Total Carbs: 19.0g | Protein: 3.8g.

Peanut Butter Banana

This athletic smoothie will give you plenty of protein and electrolytes for endurance.

___

INGREDIENTS

- 1/4 cup tofu
- 1/4 cup milk (almond, rice or soy milk is ok)
- 2 tablespoons peanut butter
- 1/2 banana (frozen)

DIRECTIONS

1. Add sweetener to taste if desired. We recommend honey or blackstrap molasses .
2. Place all of the ingredients in your blender, and blend for about 30 seconds, or until desired consistency is reached.

Nutritional Info: Calories: 158 | Sodium: 92mg | Dietary Fiber: 20g | Total Fat: 10.1g | Total Carbs: 11.9g | Protein: 7.9g.

CHAPTER 19
Stress

Banana-Berry

This is a simple smoothie, but highly effective for stress management. The potassium, magnesium and zinc from the peanut butter and banana, plus all the vitamin C and antioxidants from the berries, can reduce feelings of stress significantly.

INGREDIENTS

1/2 banana (frozen if possible)
1/4 cup berries (your choice)
1/4 cup ice cubes
1/4 cup almond or soy milk
1 tablespoons honey
1 tablespoon peanut butter

DIRECTIONS

1. Place all of the ingredients in your blender, and blend for about 30 seconds, or until desired consistency is reached.

Nutritional Info: Calories: 184 | Sodium: 39mg | Dietary Fiber: 3.4g | Total Fat: 10.1g | Total Carbs: 21.7g | Protein: 5.0g.

Grapefruit-Kale

SERVINGS: 1

Stress be gone! The potassium, magnesium, iron and vitamins A, C, B6 and D in the bananas alone are powerful stress relievers. When working together with grapefruit, kale and coconut oil, the added vitamins and minerals can combat any stress in your life.

INGREDIENTS

- 1/4 grapefruit (peeled, chopped and pitted)
- 1/2 banana
- 1 tablespoons honey
- 1/2 cup kale or spinach or romaine lettuce
- 1/4 cup ice cubes
- 1 tablespoons coconut oil
- 1/2 cup spring water

DIRECTIONS

1. Place all of the ingredients in your blender, and blend for about 30 seconds, or until desired consistency is reached.

Nutritional Info: Calories: 130 | Sodium: 9mg | Dietary Fiber: 1.2g | Total Fat: 6.9g | Total Carbs: 19g | Protein: 0.9g.

Mint-Fennel-Pineapple

SERVINGS: 1

Besides all of the vitamins and minerals in each ingredient, avocados especially provide B vitamins and potassium which helps lower blood pressure. Fennel is also a great substance, that aids in digestion and increases feelings of calmness.

INGREDIENTS

- 1/4-ounce fresh mint, chopped
- 1/4 avocado, sliced
- 1/4 cup fennel, chopped
- 1/4 cup pineapple, sliced (crushed from can is also OK)
- 1/2 cup spring water
- 1/4 cup ice cubes

DIRECTIONS

1. Place all of the ingredients in your blender, and blend for about 30 seconds, or until desired consistency is reached.

Nutritional Info: Calories: 67 | Sodium: 9.5mg | Dietary Fiber: 2.6g | Total Fat: 4.9g | Total Carbs: 5.9g | Protein: 0.9g.

CHAPTER 20
Weight Loss

Apple Pie

Just as filling and delicious as apple pie, this smoothie will keep you feeling full and satisfied, all while tasting delicious. You won't even know the difference.

INGREDIENTS

- 6 ounces plain or vanilla low-fat yogurt
- 1/2 cup of low-fat milk or soymilk
- 1 teaspoon apple pie spice
- 1 sliced apple (use your favorite kind)
- 2 tablespoons almond or cashew butter
- 4 ice cubes

DIRECTIONS

1. Place all of the ingredients in your blender, and blend for about 30 seconds, or until desired consistency is reached.

Nutritional Info: Calories: 260 | Sodium: 126mg | Dietary Fiber: 3.5g | Total Fat: 5.8g | Total Carbs: 47g | Protein: 8.1g.

Avocado Fiesta

This refreshing fusion of citrus and avocado will fill you up and energize you. It also enhances and supports your immune system and fights off infections.

INGREDIENTS

- 3/4 cups orange juice
- 3/4 cups strawberry or raspberry juice
- 1 peeled and very ripe avocados
- 6 tablespoons frozen strawberries or raspberries
- 1 tablespoon sweetener of your choice

DIRECTIONS

1. Place all of the ingredients in your blender, and blend for about 30 seconds, or until desired consistency is reached.

Nutritional Info: Calories: 68.5 | Sodium: 1.5mg | Dietary Fiber: 2.4g | Total Fat: 0.4g | Total Carbs: 17.5g | Protein: 1.0g.

Avocado - Swiss Chard

Avocado has so many nutrients that are good for you, and it helps keep you full for hours at a time. It has Selenium, Zinc, Iron and plenty of B vitamins, along with vitamins A, C and E. You also get a lot of fiber from the flaxseeds and other ingredients, which will flush out toxins and keep your lower abdomen feeling less bloated.

INGREDIENTS

- 1/2 cup Swiss chard, chopped
- 1/4 avocado, sliced
- 1/2 banana
- 1 tablespoons lemon juice
- 1/8 cup fresh mint, chopped
- 1/2 tablespoon flaxseeds, ground
- 1/4 cup soy milk
- 1/4 cup ice cubes
- 1/2 cup spring water

DIRECTIONS

1. Place all of the ingredients in your blender, and blend for about 30 seconds, or until desired consistency is reached.

Nutritional Info: Calories: 109 | Sodium: 42mg | Dietary Fiber: 3.7g | Total Fat: 6.2g | Total Carbs: 12.3g | Protein: 2.6g.

Banana - Choco Split

SERVINGS: 2

This smoothie tastes delicious, is full of protein and nutrients, and still remains low in calories. It will give you that full feeling that will help you not to want to snack.

INGREDIENTS

- 1/8 cup cocoa powder (or chocolate syrup)
- 3/4 bananas
- 6 tablespoons tofu
- 3/4 cups low fat milk or soy milk
- 1 1/2 tablespoons proffered sweetener

DIRECTIONS

1. Place all of the ingredients in your blender, and blend for about 30 seconds, or until desired consistency is reached.

Nutritional Info: Calories: 123 | Sodium: 48mg | Dietary Fiber: 4.0g | Total Fat: 3.7g | Total Carbs: 20.2g | Protein: 8.4g.

Banana Peanut Butter Delight

This smoothie is a great low-calorie meal replacer, and full of vitamins, minerals and protein. It will fill you with lots of energy.

INGREDIENTS

- 1/2 banana
- 10 tablespoons low fat milk (or soy milk)
- 3 1/2 tablespoons smooth peanut butter (preferably low fat)
- 1 tablespoons protein powder
- 4 ice cubes

DIRECTIONS

1. Place all of the ingredients in your blender, and blend for about 30 seconds, or until desired consistency is reached.

Nutritional Info: Calories: 371 | Sodium: 83mg | Dietary Fiber: 3.3g | Total Fat: 23.4g | Total Carbs: 20.7g | Protein: 24.8g.

Berry Berry Yummy

SERVINGS: 1

The mixed berries in this smoothie provide plenty of antioxidants, while the yogurt and protein powder strengthen your body with essential protein.

INGREDIENTS

- 3/4 cups frozen mixed berries
- 1/4 banana
- 3 ice cubes
- 3/4 cups plain or vanilla low fat yogurt (can be substituted with low fat milk)
- 1/2 tablespoon sweetener of choice

DIRECTIONS

1. Place all of the ingredients in your blender, and blend for about 30 seconds, or until desired consistency is reached.

Nutritional Info: Calories: 115 | Sodium: 50mg | Dietary Fiber: 2.5g | Total Fat: 1.0g | Total Carbs: 25g | Protein: 2.8g.

Blue Smoothie

Blueberries contain natural antioxidants and plenty of vitamins and essential minerals, such as iron, manganese, calcium and copper. The recipe below is a delicious, low calorie drink that will keep you feeling full.

INGREDIENTS

3 1/2 tablespoons soy protein
1/2 large banana
1/4 cup frozen blueberries
1/2 tablespoon flaxseed oil
8 ounces water
1/2 tablespoon honey (or sweetener of choice)
3 ice cubes (optional)

DIRECTIONS

1. Place all of the ingredients in your blender, and blend for about 30 seconds, or until desired consistency is reached.

Nutritional Info: Calories: 111 | Sodium: 36mg | Dietary Fiber: 1.6g | Total Fat: 0.0g | Total Carbs: 17.3g | Protein: 1.9g.

Cashew Banana

This smoothie is perfect for weight loss and will keep you feeling full.

INGREDIENTS

- 1 tablespoons cashew butter
- 3/4 bananas
- 1/2 tablespoon flaxseed oil
- 1/2 cup low fat plain or vanilla yogurt
- 1 1/2 tablespoons sweetener of choice
- 1/2 tablespoon vanilla extract.

DIRECTIONS

1. Place all of the ingredients in your blender, and blend for about 30 seconds, or until desired consistency is reached.

Nutritional Info: Calories: 175 | Sodium: 32mg | Dietary Fiber: 2.2g | Total Fat: 8.2g | Total Carbs: 22.1g | Protein: 4.5g.

Citrus Joy

Both tangy and sweet, this smoothie will satisfy your hunger and keep you energized for hours.

INGREDIENTS

6 ounces citrus flavored yogurt (of choice)
1 orange cut into pieces
3/4 cups soymilk or low-fat milk
3/4 tablespoons flaxseed oil
4 ice cubes

DIRECTIONS

1. Place all of the ingredients in your blender, and blend for about 30 seconds, or until desired consistency is reached.

Nutritional Info: Calories: 197 | Sodium: 104mg | Dietary Fiber: 2.8g | Total Fat: 4.8g | Total Carbs: 26.1g | Protein: 6.4g.

Grab Bag

Use the fruit you have on hand and combine with a few other ingredients for a delicious and satisfying drink. The apples and oranges below can be substituted with any fruit of choice.

INGREDIENTS

- 1/2 banana
- 1/4 cup apple slices
- 3/4 oranges (peeled and sectioned)
- 1 1/2 tablespoons honey (or your choice of sweetener)
- 4 ice cubes
- 1/2 cup low-fat milk or soymilk

DIRECTIONS

1. Place all of the ingredients in your blender, and blend for about 30 seconds, or until desired consistency is reached.

Nutritional Info: Calories: 391 | Sodium: 251mg | Dietary Fiber: 5.9g | Total Fat: 8.5g | Total Carbs: 63.1g | Protein: 17.0g.

Hawaiian Supreme

This low calorie and high fiber smoothie is the perfect meal to feel full and avoid snacking.

INGREDIENTS

- 4 ounces pineapple chunks with juice (canned is fine)
- 3/4 cups low fat milk or soymilk
- 1 tablespoons flaxseed oil
- 4 ice cubes
- 1 1/2 tablespoons sweetener of choice

DIRECTIONS

1. Place all of the ingredients in your blender, and blend for about 30 seconds, or until desired consistency is reached.

Nutritional Info: Calories: 132 | Sodium: 55mg | Dietary Fiber: 1.7g | Total Fat: 7.9g | Total Carbs: 13.7g | Protein: 3.4g.

Kale-Ginger

SERVINGS: 1

Kale is one of the most nutritious leafy greens out there, full of vitamins C and K, beta carotene, and with plenty of antioxidants. Kale is also a great detoxifier, which means it helps the body rid itself of toxins. This is good for weight loss and reducing the risk of cancer. Ginger aids in digestion and gastrointestinal problems, and now many people are adding it to their weight loss regimens with great success.

INGREDIENTS

- 1 cup kale or spinach or romaine lettuce
- 1 apple, peeled, sliced and seeded
- 1/4 bunch parsley
- 1/2 cucumber, peeled and sliced
- 1 celery stalk, chopped
- 1/2 lemon, peeled, sliced and seeded
- 2 teaspoons ginger, chopped
- 1 cup spring water

DIRECTIONS

1. Place all of the ingredients in your blender, and blend for about 30 seconds, or until desired consistency is reached.

Nutritional Info: Calories: 187 | Sodium: 82mg | Dietary Fiber: 8.9g | Total Fat: 1.2g | Total Carbs: 44.4g | Protein: 5.7g.

Hot Tomato

SERVINGS: 1

This smoothie is a Bloody Mary without the alcohol or negative side effects. Get energized with a natural dose of vitamins and minerals .

INGREDIENTS

- 1/4 cup apple juice
- 1/2 cup tomato juice
- 3/4 cups chopped tomatoes
- 3 1/2 tablespoons chopped carrots
- 3 1/2 tablespoons chopped celery
- 1/3 teaspoons hot sauce
- 5 ice cubes

DIRECTIONS

1. Place all of the ingredients in your blender, and blend for about 30 seconds, or until desired consistency is reached.

Nutritional Info: Calories: 48 | Sodium: 230mg | Dietary Fiber: 1.8g | Total Fat: 0.25g | Total Carbs: 11.1g | Protein: 1.4g.

Key Lime

Tangy, delicious, low calorie and full of vitamin C.

INGREDIENTS

- 6 tablespoons sliced and peeled lime
- 3/4 cups low fat milk or soy milk
- 3/4 cups lime sherbet
- 1/3 cups strawberries
- 4 ice cubes

DIRECTIONS

1. Place all of the ingredients in your blender, and blend for about 30 seconds, or until desired consistency is reached.

Nutritional Info: Calories: 265 | Sodium: 104mg | Dietary Fiber: 1.7g | Total Fat: 3.5g | Total Carbs: 53g | Protein: 8.2g.

Mango Bliss

SERVINGS: 1

Mangos are tasty, sweet and full of vitamins C, A and B6. They also have lots of natural fiber which keeps you feeling full and reduces the risk of colon cancer.

INGREDIENTS

- 1/2 cup mango juice
- 1 tablespoon sweetener of choice
- 1 tablespoon lime or lemon juice
- 3 ice cubes
- 1/4 cup mashed ripe avocado
- 1/4 cup plain or vanilla low-fat yogurt
- 1/4 cup mangoes, cubed

DIRECTIONS

1. Place all of the ingredients in your blender, and blend for about 30 seconds, or until desired consistency is reached.

Nutritional Info: Calories: 105 | Sodium: 37mg | Dietary Fiber: 2.7g | Total Fat: 3.9g | Total Carbs: 18.8g | Protein: 1.4g.

Melon Perfection

SERVINGS: 1

This smoothie is extremely low calorie and will give you energy for hours.

INGREDIENTS

- 1 1/2 cups cantaloupe, chopped
- 3/4 cups raspberries or strawberries (frozen or fresh)
- 4 ice cubes
- 3/4 cups chopped Romaine lettuce leaves

DIRECTIONS

1. Place all of the ingredients in your blender, and blend for about 30 seconds, or until desired consistency is reached.

Nutritional Info: Calories: 65 | Sodium: 34.5mg | Dietary Fiber: 3.9g | Total Fat: 0.3g | Total Carbs: 15.2g | Protein: 1.4g.

Mocha Espresso Wake Up

SERVINGS: 1

This low calorie, high-energy smoothie will wake you up and keep you full for hours. This drink is filled with antioxidants, protein and caffeine for an energized morning.

INGREDIENTS

- 2 teaspoons cocoa powder
- 1 shot espresso
- 1/2 cup low-fat plain or vanilla yogurt
- 1 tablespoon chia seeds
- 1 tablespoon sweetener of choice
- 3 ice cubes

DIRECTIONS

1. Place all of the ingredients in your blender, and blend for about 30 seconds, or until desired consistency is reached.

Nutritional Info: Calories: 128 | Sodium: 54mg | Dietary Fiber: 6.4g | Total Fat: 6.2g | Total Carbs: 12.2g | Protein: 7.0g.

Peachy Keen

Peaches are quite refreshing, and they provide plenty of energy. The chia seeds in this recipe will keep you full for hours.

INGREDIENTS

- 3/4 cups sliced frozen or fresh peaches
- 1/2 tablespoon chia seeds
- 3/4 cups low fat or non-fat milk
- 2 ice cubes
- 1 1/2 tablespoons sweetener of choice

DIRECTIONS

1. Place all of the ingredients in your blender, and blend for about 30 seconds, or until desired consistency is reached.

Nutritional Info: Calories: 97 | Sodium: 62mg | Dietary Fiber: 4.5g | Total Fat: 2.6g | Total Carbs: 15g | Protein: 5.1g.

Raspberry Treat

Raspberries are rich in minerals such as potassium, copper, iron, manganese and magnesium, and high in vitamins K and B-complex. These vitamins are extremely helpful for boosting our metabolism, which leads to weight-loss. The dark chocolate in the recipe adds extra antioxidants.

INGREDIENTS

- 5 ounces plain or vanilla low-fat yogurt
- 1/2 cup low fat, skim milk or soymilk
- 1/4 cup dark chocolate chips
- 3/4 cups raspberries (frozen or fresh)
- 3/4 cups raspberry juice
- 3 ice cubes

DIRECTIONS

1. Place all of the ingredients in your blender, and blend for about 30 seconds, or until desired consistency is reached.

Nutritional Info: Calories: 278 | Sodium: 112mg | Dietary Fiber: 3.3g | Total Fat: 7.1g | Total Carbs: 51.1g | Protein: 7.3g.

Red Banana

SERVINGS: 1

Bananas fill you up while providing essential nutrients such as magnesium, potassium, copper and vitamin B6. These nutrients promote bone and heart health, and regulate blood pressure.

INGREDIENTS

3 ice cubes
1/4 cup apple, orange or juice of your choice
3/4 bananas
3/4 cups strawberries
1/2 sliced orange
1/2 cup low fat plain or vanilla yogurt

DIRECTIONS

1. Place all of the ingredients in your blender, and blend for about 30 seconds, or until desired consistency is reached.

Nutritional Info: Calories: 136 | Sodium: 55mg | Dietary Fiber: 3/4g | Total Fat: 1.2g | Total Carbs: 27.2g | Protein: 4.9g.

Strawberry Spinach

SERVINGS: 1

This delicious low-calorie smoothie is loaded with protein, vitamins and minerals.

INGREDIENTS

- 1/4 banana
- 1/8 cup orange juice
- 1/8 cup strawberries (frozen or fresh)
- 3 ounces plain or vanilla yogurt
- 1/4 cup spinach
- 2 baby carrots
- 1/8 cup protein powder
- 1/2 teaspoon flaxseed oil
- 2 ice cubes
- 1/2 tablespoon dry oatmeal

DIRECTIONS

1. Place all of the ingredients in your blender, and blend for about 30 seconds, or until desired consistency is reached.

Nutritional Info: Calories: 103 | Sodium: 78mg | Dietary Fiber: 1.1g | Total Fat: 2.3g | Total Carbs: 11.9g | Protein: 8.4g.

Tooty-Fruity

This smoothie is a great tasting low calorie option that will keep you energized.

INGREDIENTS

1 frozen banana
3/4 cups peach slices (frozen or fresh)
1/4 cup blueberries (or strawberries)
1/2 cup low fat plain or vanilla yogurt
1 tablespoon protein powder
1/4 cup low fat milk or soymilk

DIRECTIONS

1. Place all of the ingredients in your blender, and blend for about 30 seconds, or until desired consistency is reached.

Nutritional Info: Calories: 232 | Sodium: 194mg | Dietary Fiber: 1.9g | Total Fat: 3.7g | Total Carbs: 32g | Protein: 17.3g.

CHAPTER 21
Kids

Ice Cream-Less

SERVINGS: 1

This smoothie tastes wonderful without ice cream, proving that eating healthy can be a tasty endeavor. This recipe offers plenty of vitamins, minerals and protein for growing bodies and minds.

INGREDIENTS

1/2 mango (pitted and sliced)
1/2 cup soy milk
1/4 cup ice cubes
1/4 banana

DIRECTIONS

1. Place all of the ingredients in your blender, and blend for about 30 seconds, or until desired consistency is reached.

Nutritional Info: Calories: 83 | Sodium: 34mg | Dietary Fiber: 1.7g | Total Fat: 1.25g | Total Carbs: 16g | Protein: 2.4g.

Peanut Butter Madness

SERVINGS: 1

Try out this delicious kid-friendly recipe as a slightly healthier alternative to an ice cream sundae. If desired, substitute the ice cream with a frozen soy dessert.

INGREDIENTS

- 1/4 cup vanilla ice cream
- 1/8 cup natural peanut butter
- 1/2 cup milk (soy or almond milk is ok)
- 1/4 cup ice cubes

DIRECTIONS

1. Place all of the ingredients in your blender, and blend for about 30 seconds, or until desired consistency is reached.

Nutritional Info: Calories: 166 | Sodium: 47mg | Dietary Fiber: 1.1g | Total Fat: 11.2g | Total Carbs: 10.3g | Protein: 7.8g.

The Hybrid

SERVINGS: 1

Your kids will never guess that there are leafy greens in this delicious smoothie. This recipe offers plenty of vitamin C, antioxidants, and protein to keep your child happy and healthy.

INGREDIENTS

- 1/4 cup spring water
- 1/4 cup orange juice
- 1/4 cup strawberries
- 1/4 cup blueberries
- 1/2 cup kale or spinach (chopped)

DIRECTIONS

1. Place all of the ingredients in your blender, and blend for about 30 seconds, or until desired consistency is reached.

Nutritional Info: Calories: 38 | Sodium: 8mg | Dietary Fiber: 1.1g | Total Fat: 0.2g | Total Carbs: 9.0g | Protein: 1.0g.

NEXT STEPS...

ABOUT THE AUTHOR

Lisa Brian is a San Francisco Bay Area-based health writer and chef who has been blending superfood smoothies since she was a little girl.

Living an active lifestyle in health-oriented Marin, she's always on the lookout for new and exciting foods to put into her blender. If they maximize nutrition and tastiness, she'll try the new recipe on some friends, and eventually publish the recipes which make it through her various popularity tests.

Check out her upcoming blog on superfood smoothies and Ninja Blender tech (soon to be announced :).

Want a Personal 24/7 Cooking Coach?

Learn New Recipes & Techniques for FREE!

Get Access Now!
Go to www.CookingCoach.online
or use this QR code: